Bigger

This  is **big**. This  is **bigger**.

Look at the pictures in each row.
Circle the picture that is **bigger** than the first picture.

Smaller

This  is **small**. This  is **smaller**.

Look at the pictures in each row.
Circle the picture that is **smaller** than the first picture.

Same Size

These  are the **same size**.

Look at the pictures in each box.
Circle the pictures that are the **same size**.

What Is a Square?

A **square** is a **shape** that looks like this. □

How many □s can you find? ______

What Is a Rectangle?

A **rectangle** is a **shape** that looks like this. ▭

How many ▭s can you find? ______

What Is a Circle?

A **circle** is a **shape** that looks like this. 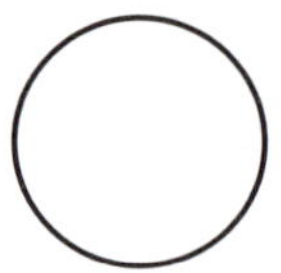

How many ◯s can you find? ______

What Is a Triangle?

A **triangle** is a **shape** that looks like this. 

How many △s can you find? ______

Different

These  are the **same**. This  is **different**.

Look at the pictures in each row.
Circle the picture that is **different**.

Different

Look at the pictures in each row. Circle the picture that is **different**.

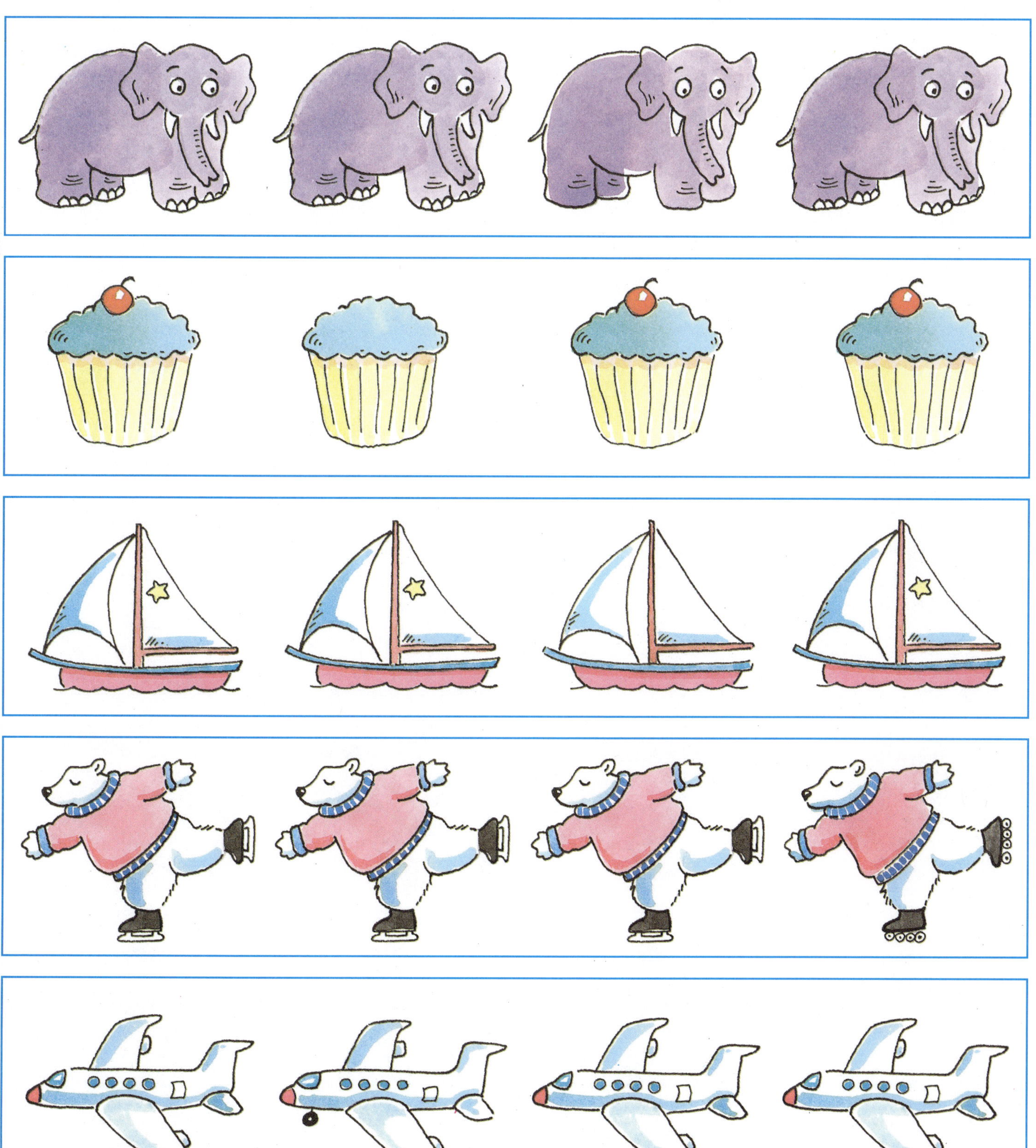

What Belongs?

A and **belong** together.

Look at the pictures in each row.
Circle the picture that **belongs** with the first picture.

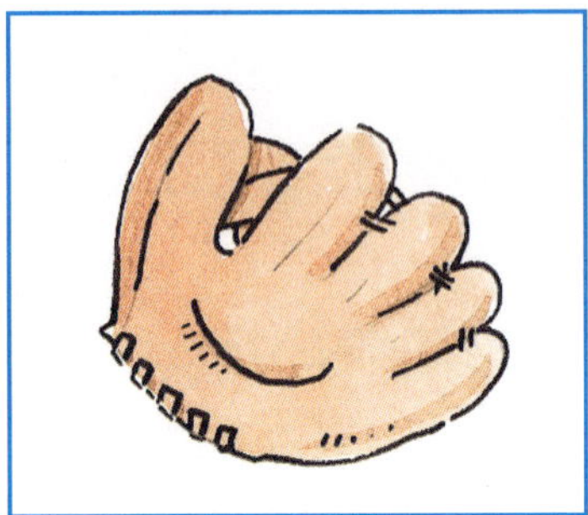  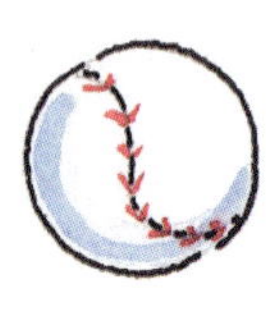 

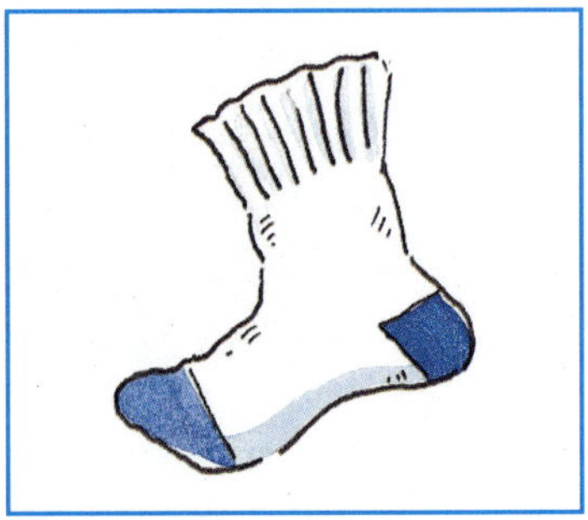   

What Belongs?

Draw a line from the  below to the pictures that **belong** with it.

What Belongs?

Draw a line from the 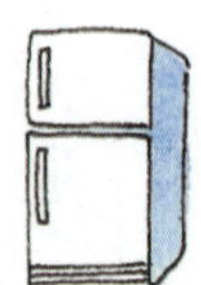 below to what **belongs** in it.

What Belongs?

Where does each animal **belong**?
Draw a line from each animal to its house.

Make a Pair

A  and a  make a **pair**.

A  and a  do not make a **pair**.

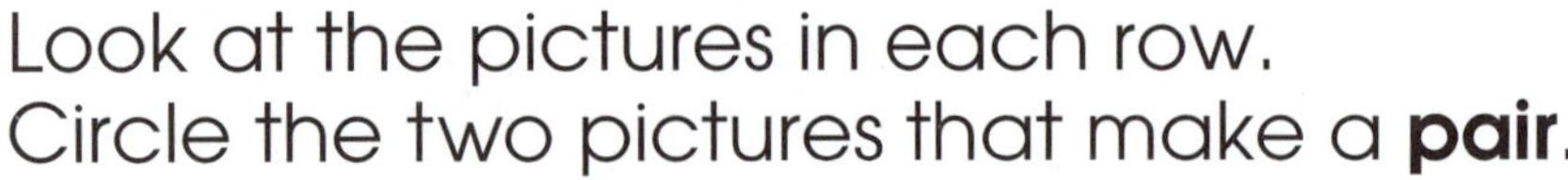

Look at the pictures in each row.
Circle the two pictures that make a **pair**.

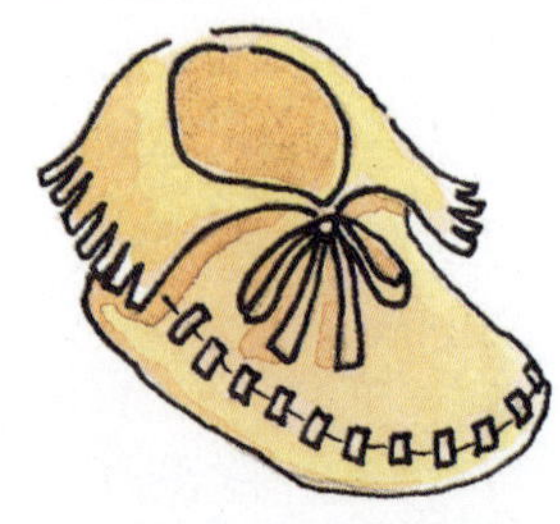   

Make a Pair

A  and a  make a **pair**.

A  and a  do not make a **pair**.

Look at the pictures in each row.
Circle the two pictures that make a **pair**.

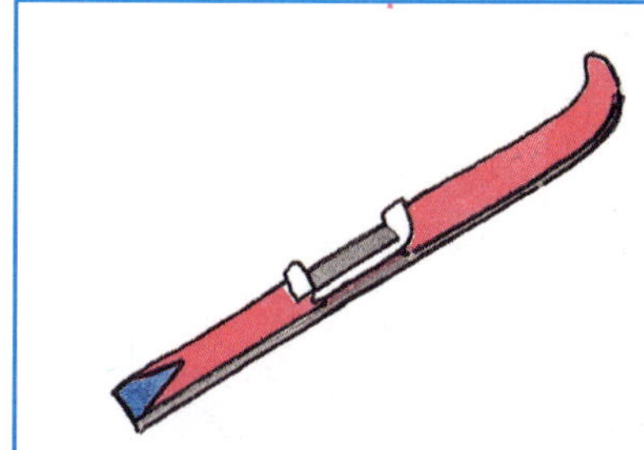   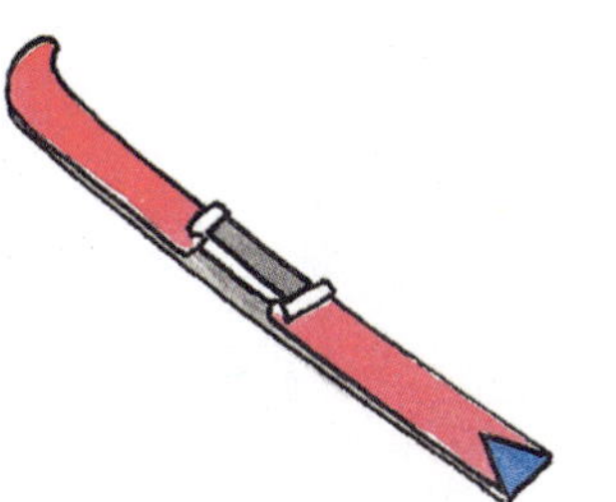

  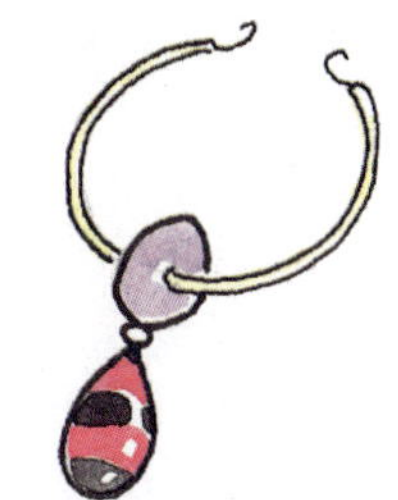 

What Is Missing?

Look at the picture.
Then look for the **missing** parts.
Draw in each where it belongs.

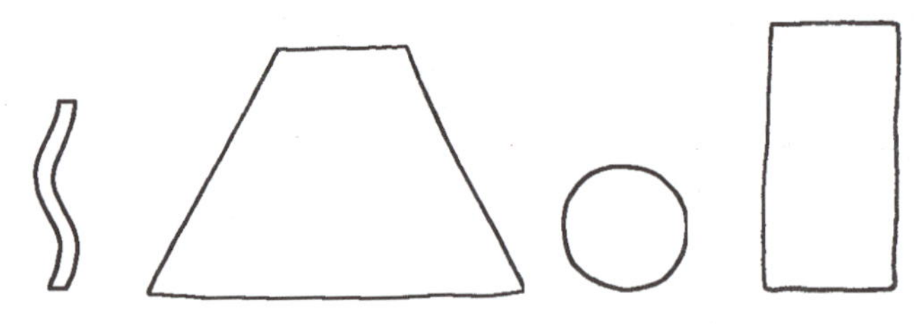

What Is Missing?

Look at the picture.
Then look for the **missing** parts.
Draw in each where it belongs.

Opposites

This  is happy. This  is sad.

Happy is the **opposite** of sad.

Draw a line from each word to the picture of its **opposite**.

little

night

up

Opposites

Circle the picture that shows the **opposite** of the first picture.

big

soft

full

hot

Rhyming

rhymes with

.

Say the name of each picture.
Circle the two that **rhyme** in each group.

Rhyming

This  is a hen.

Draw a line from the  below to the picture names that **rhyme**.

Which Is Less Than?

Less means **not as many**. 7 is **less than** 8.

Look at the pictures in each row. Circle the set that is **less**.

Make a set of  s to show 1 **less than** 10.

How many ♥s? ______

Which Is Greater Than?

Greater means **more than.** 8 is **greater than** 7.

Look at the pictures in each row. Circle the set that is **greater**.

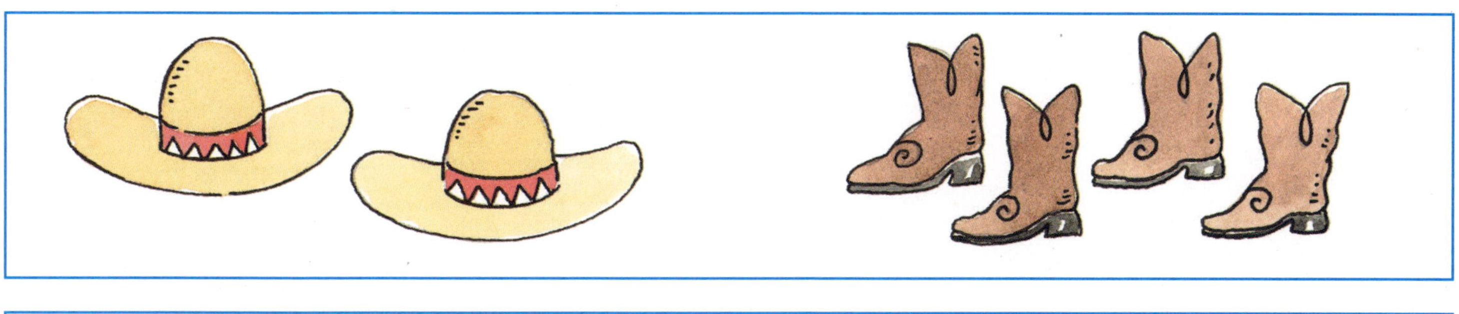

Make a set of  s to show 1 **more than** 3.

How many s? ______

First, Next, Last

Write **1** in the square to show what happened **first**.
Write **2** to show what happened **next**.
Write **3** to show what happened **last**.

First, Next, Last

Write **1** in the square to show what happened **first**.
Write **2** to show what happened **next**.
Write **3** to show what happened **last**.

First, Next, Last

Write **1** in the square to show what happened **first**.
Write **2** to show what happened **next**.
Write **3** to show what happened **last**.

Before

A comes **before** B.

Write the letter that comes **before** each letter below.

A B C D E F G H I J K L M N O P Q R S T U V W X Y Z

Between

B comes **between** A and C.

Write each letter that comes **between** the letters below.

A B C D E F G H I J K L M N O P Q R S T U V W X Y Z

After

C comes **after** B.

Write the letter that comes **after** each letter below.

A B C D E F G H I J K L M N O P Q R S T U V W X Y Z

Letter Match

Look at the ball players. Draw a line from each **uppercase** letter to the matching **lowercase** letter.

A B C D E F G H I J K L M N O P Q R S T U V W X Y Z

a b c d e f g h i j k l m n o p q r s t u v w x y z

B

r

Q

b

R

q

Letter Match

Write the matching **lowercase** letter next to each **uppercase** letter.

A B C D E F G H I J K L M N O P Q R S T U V W X Y Z

a b c d e f g h i j k l m n o p q r s t u v w x y z

Letter Match

Draw a line from each **uppercase** letter to the **lowercase** letter that matches.

Fill in the Letters

Fill in each blank with the letter that comes **next** in ABC order.

What Order?

Write each set of letters in **ABC order**.

Fill in the Letters

Fill in each blank with the letter that comes **next** in ABC order.

Beginning Sounds

Say the name of each picture.
Write **t** or **n** to begin the word.
Then write the word on the line.

___op

___ent

___est

___ut

Beginning Sounds

Say the name of each picture.
Write **m** or **p** to begin the word.
Then write the word on the line.

___oon

___ig

___an

___an

Ending Sounds

Say the name of each picture.
Write **d** or **t** to end the word.
Then write the word on the line.

be__

goa__

ca__

bir__

Ending Sounds

Say the name of each picture.
Write **m** or **n** to end the word.
Then write the word on the line.

su__

gu__

dru__

fa__

First, Next, Last

Write **1** in the square to show what happened **first**.
Write **2** to show what happened **next**.
Write **3** to show what happened **last**.

First, Next, Last

Write **1** in the square to show what happened **first**.
Write **2** to show what happened **next**.
Write **3** to show what happened **last**.

Which Two Go Together?

Draw a line from each **little** picture to the correct **big** picture.

Circle the names of the pictures in each row that **go together**.

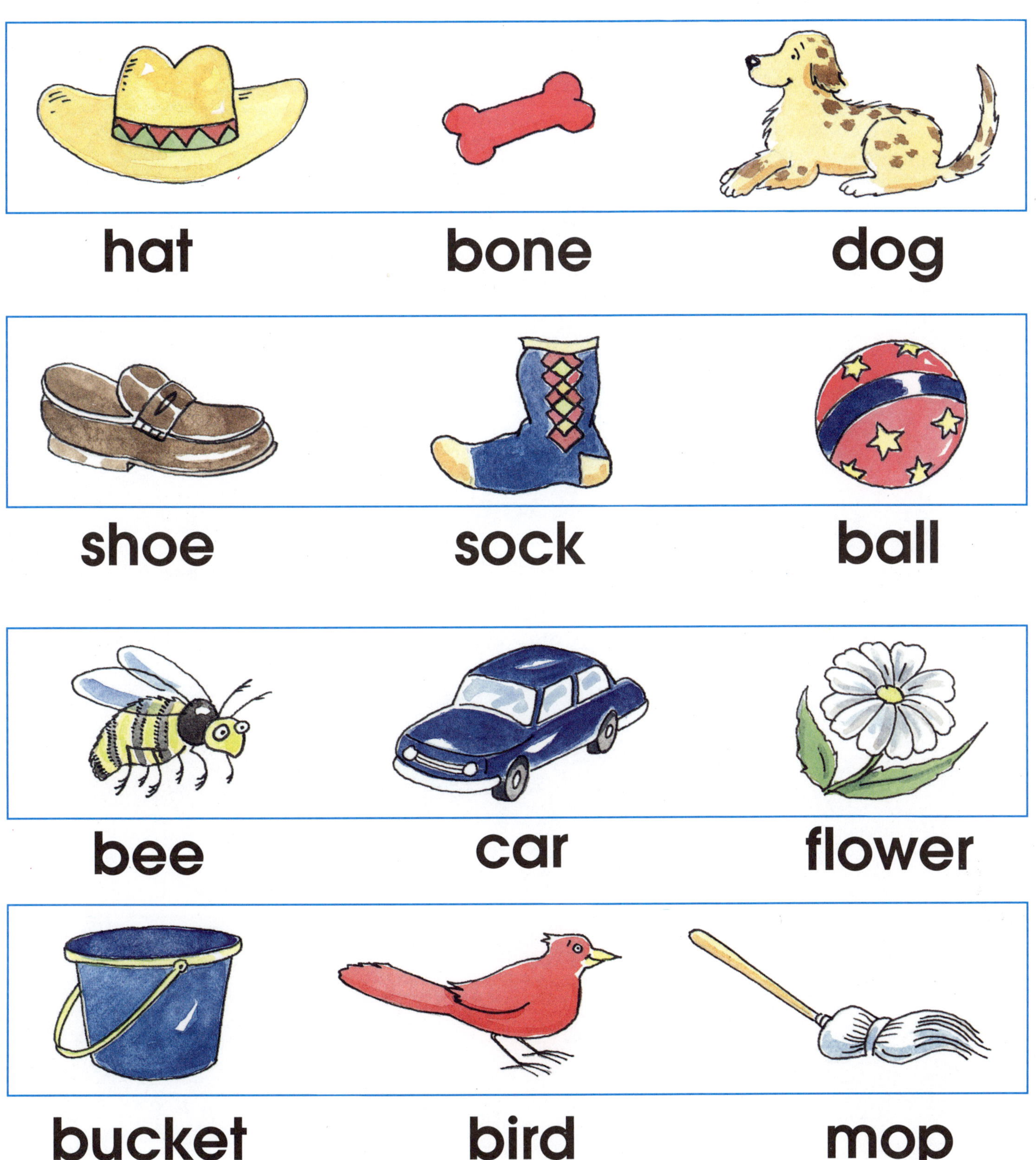

One Does Not Belong

Circle the name of the picture in each row that **does not belong**.

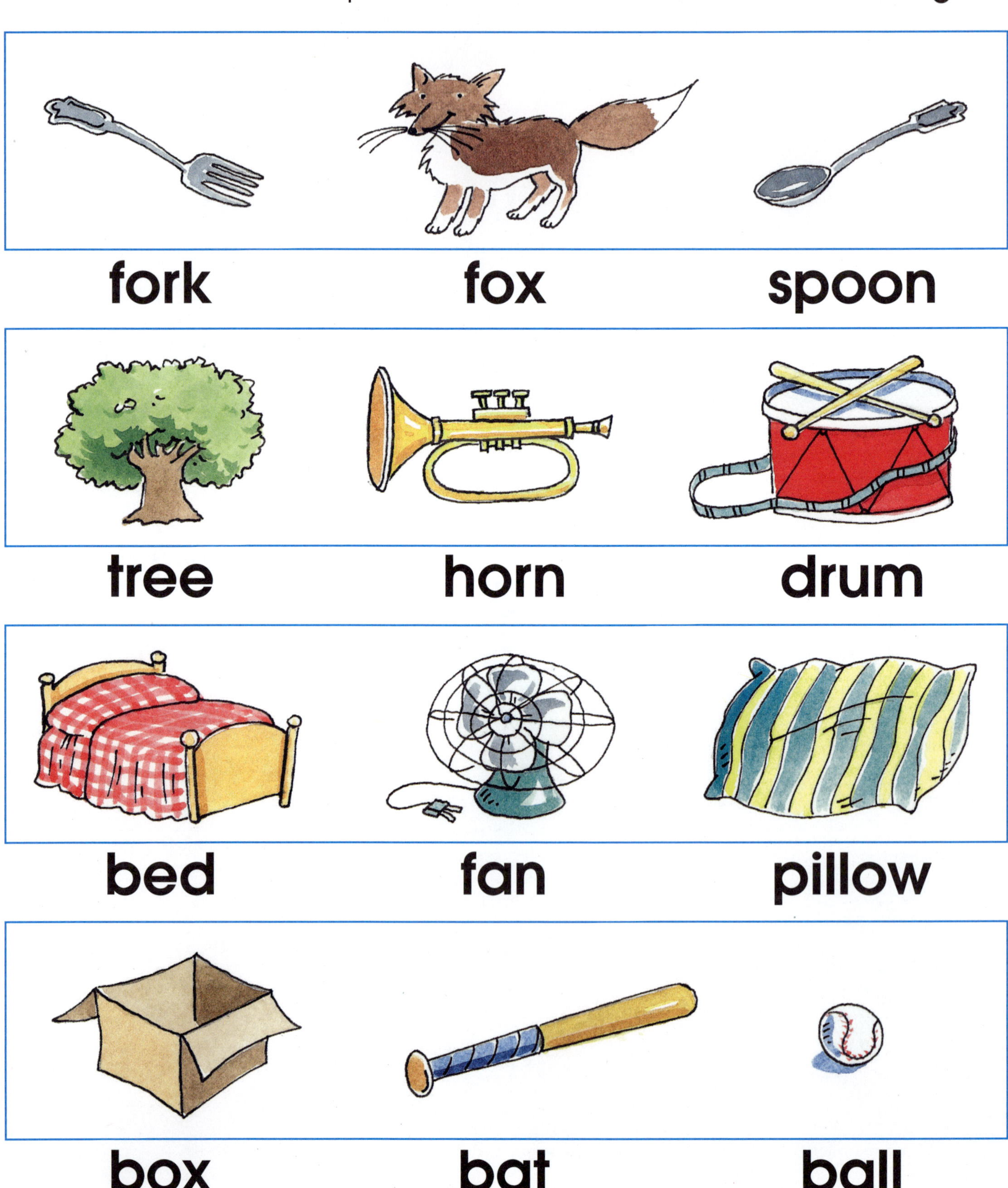

One Does Not Belong

Circle the name of the picture in each row that **does not belong**.

Number Words

Colour **two** ☆s yellow.

Colour **three** UFOs red.

Colour **four** planets blue.

Colour **one** alien green.

Draw a ◯ around the set of **7**.

Draw a ☐ around the set of **6**.

eight

seven

nine

six

ten

Colour the Picture

Colour the  **green**.

Colour the  **yellow**.

Colour the  **blue**.

Colour the  **purple**.

Colour the **orange**.

Colour the **brown**.

Colour the **red**.

Colour the **black**.

Leave the **white**.

Words That Rhyme

Draw a ◯ around the words that **rhyme** with **sing**.

Draw a ☐ around the words that **rhyme** with **ran**.

Draw a ○ around the words that **rhyme** with **sat**.

Draw a □ around the words that **rhyme** with **lake**.

Which Is It?

Write the names of the **animals** on the **left**.
Write the names of the **plants** on the **right**.

Where Does It Belong?

Draw a line from the **foods** to the  .

Draw a line from the **toys** to the  .

apple

berry

doll

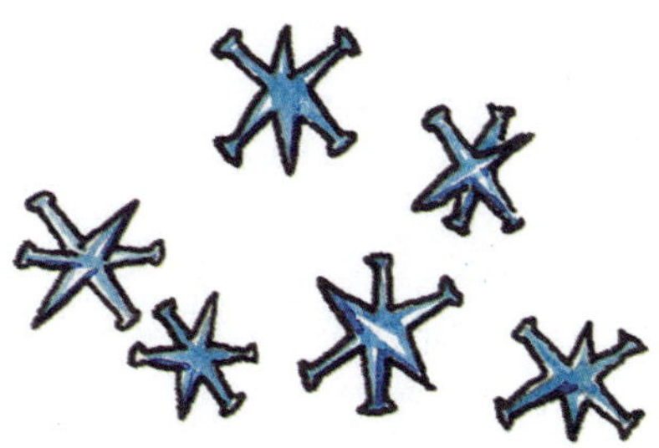

jacks

ball

cake

Words

Draw a line from each word to the picture it names.

man

jam

pan

fan

ham

Words

Draw a line from each picture to its name.

hen

goat

men

boat

pen

Where Is It?

over

by

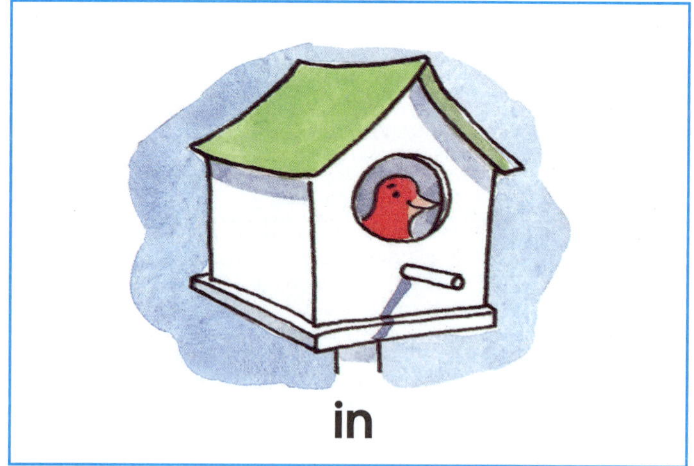
in

under

Write the word that tells **where** the bird is.

The bird is ______________ the  **.**

The bird is ______________ the .

The bird is ______________ the .

The bird is ______________ the .

Where Is It?

Draw a red apple **under** the table.

Draw a green apple **on** the table.

Draw a yellow apple **by** the table.

In, On and Under

Write the correct **number** on each line.

 How many s are **under** the ? ______

How many s are **in** the  ? ______

How many  s are **on** the  ? ______

Alphabetical Order

Write the words in **ABC order**.

apple

a b c d e f g h i j k l m n o p q r s t u v w x y z

Write the words in **ABC order**.

car

a b c d e f g h i j k l m n o p q r s t u v w x y z

What Do You See?

Underline the sentence that **goes with** each picture.

See the ball.

See the dog.

See the doll.

See the ball.

See the boat.

See the dog.

See the doll.

See the boat.

Underline the sentences that tell what you see.

There are two cows.

There are four balls.

There is a house.

There is one goat.

There is a girl.

First Name: ______________________

Last Name: ______________________

has completed **Reading Readiness**